A *Potpourri*
of POEMS

GARY TEN EYCK, PE

iUniverse®

A POTPOURRI OF POEMS GARY TEN EYCK, PE

iUniverse books may be ordered through booksellers or by contacting:

iUniverse
1663 Liberty Drive
Bloomington, IN 47403
www.iuniverse.com
1-800-Authors (1-800-288-4677)

Because of the dynamic nature of the internet, any web addresses or links contained in this book may have changed since publication and may no longer be valid. The views expressed in this work are solely those of the author and do not necessarily reflect the views of the publisher, and the publisher hereby disclaims any responsibility for them.

Any people depicted in stock imagery provided by Getty Images are models, and such images are being used for illustrative purposes only. Certain stock imagery © Getty Images.

ISBN: 978-1-5320-4322-2 (sc)
ISBN: 978-1-5320-4324-6 (hc)
ISBN: 978-1-5320-4323-9 (e)

Library of Congress Control Number: 2018904075

Print information available on the last page.

iUniverse rev. date: 05/10/2018

Contents

I want to acknowledge and thank my daughter, Erica Ten Eyck Paceleo, for all her work in typing my entire book, including editing and correcting this poet's errors and omissions. Without her hard and dedicated work, this book would not have been completed. Thank you, my dear and darling daughter.

—Dad

Reflections on Life and Love in My World

Two Hundred Years
and the Engineers

Think about this, you engineers,
As the bicentennial time draws near.
Do we get the credit that we deserve?
I think this country has got its nerve.
It's fine to wave the flag, all right,
But there's something we should keep in sight.

We hear about the pioneers.
What about the engineers?
We know about the covered wagon,
Not the engineer who kept it from draggin'.

We know of Washington, the river, and the boat.
It was an engineer who kept him afloat.
He built the bridges to span the land;
He and God did, hand in hand.

If it wasn't for the engineers,
Things would have been different after two hundred years.
Wastewater treatments rise from the mud
To cleanse away two hundred years of crud.

To make us number one in space,
Those electronic brains helped win that race.
Skeletons of steel pierce the sky
Because a structural man continued to try.

And so you, folks of the USA,
When we think of the past this special day,
When the parade goes by, with a flood of tears,
Please pause and thank all engineers.

July 4, 1976

A Face

I saw a face on the seas,
On sun-warmed sand, on the breeze.
I saw a face in clouded skies.
I saw it smile as it kissed the trees.

This face I thought I knew quite well—
This warm, this soft, this tender shell,
Of a soul quite deep that I had yet to learn,
Of a twist, a faith I had yet to earn.

As a soft sea breeze erased the face,
A tropic sun glowed in its place.
The coming tide across the sand
Caressed this face to caress my hand.

Yes, this face was yours I saw today,
And yours—yes, yours—it will always stay.
But as nature lovingly shared with me,
I hope one day I can be with thee.

August 1985
St. Thomas, US Virgin Islands

A New Year's Thought

The end of the year is drawing near.
It's a time to pause and think—
To "reverize" through misty eyes
Over a solitary drink.

This year just past brought a love to last
And joy that I've never known.
I have a family to live with me
And a place to call my home.

With the year behind and our love in mind,
We began to plan our future.
'76 was as good as any year could be,
Our lives mended by God's suture.

I have no dread over what lies ahead.
This will be an exciting year.
The decisions we make will courage take,
And God will soothe our fear.

Will it be Spain, or a city plainer,
Like Lansing or Atlanta, G-A?
But whatever it is, in my engineering biz,
It'll be good, I can truly say.

So let's raise a glass, forget the past,
And drink to a brand-new year—
To hopes and dreams and life serene
And the love you gave me, dear.

A Snow Day

The snow came down; it covered the ground
And piled deeper and deeper and higher.
The wind whipped by and blew dust in the sky
As we crowded closer and closer to the fire.

As dawn finally came, it still snowed the same.
The earth was a mantle of white.
We were buried alive; would we survive?
It was a cold but beautiful sight.

Then the radio blared that sickening word
That makes parents' blood run cold.
"It's been proposed that schools be closed,"
Said the DJ in a voice so bold.

God, we're trapped at home with those little gnomes.
This will truly be the longest day.
They'll whine and fight and get us uptight
As they tire of games to play.

They're in and out; they scatter clothes about
And track in the slush and the snow.
Five minutes from home, and they're chilled to the bone.
My God, how the day goes slow.

Finally it's night—seems like sheer delight.
The kids are at last fast asleep.
Then the radio repeats as you fall in your seat,
"No school again; the snow's still too deep."

Circa January 1978

A Thought on Christmas

Christmastime and holiday fare,
A festive mood that fills the air—
Tinsel glitters, and lights do too.
Then why do I feel the way I do?

It seems to me with the Christmas season,
Problems appear for no apparent reason.
I don't mean bills and mundane things
But the pain and anguish that trouble brings.

In summertime when the air is warm,
Life seems so simple; thoughts will conform.
But when winter comes with darkened clouds,
The pall of life falls like a shroud.

I wonder if Christ picked the Christmas season
To be in winter for this very reason.
Maybe it was intended that man despair—
The proper way for us to prepare.

Could it be the coming of Christ indeed
Should coincide with turmoil and greed?
That the very essence of this holy thing
Was the antithesis of what evil brings?

To me, this year, with feeling drear,
With more and more problems becoming clear,
I really wonder if God was right,
Picking now for his holy night.

I hope and pray that on this special day,
God will have something more relevant to say
Than "Peace on earth, goodwill to men"
When it's obvious this won't happen again.

I hope that living through this festive season
Will give my life a living reason.
I pray that celebrating his holy birth
Will prove next year to be of some real worth.

December 1977

A Time of Stress

Don't cry, my darling.
Salvation's near.
We'll have a reprieve.
Please don't let us fear.
Things get bad;
You're awful sad.
But a month from now,
You'll be happy and glad.
I think it's time to fly away
And spend two days at Inn Holiday.

Body Language

When you scratch yer nose, or wiggle yer toes,
You think that's all you've done.
When you bite yer lip or take a trip,
You'd think it is a simple motion.

When you wiggle an ear or shed a tear,
Should it be such a grand intrigue?
It ain't so simple when you itch a pimple—
Just a sign of yer body's fatigue.

It's mind-boggling, folks, and that ain't no joke
When the learned ones say today.
Those simple motions give us a notion
Of what you really want to say.

By the time they're done, yer the only one
Who don't know what you mean.
Other folks around have yer thoughts all down.
Yer body language spilled the beans.

August 1977

Charlie's Latrine

Of all the joints I've been to before
And all the places I've seen,
The one that's foremost in my mind
Is a bar called Charlie's Latrine.

The beer is sour an' kinda warm
An' looks a little green.
But the glasses are so cloudy
That the mung just can't be seen.

Potato chips are like spongy noodles
Served in an old spittoon.
But they're so used and much abused
That ya eat 'em with a spoon.

The hamburgs are no steak divine.
With the tummy, they do battle.
But the strange thing about that tenderloin
Is they forgot to remove the saddle.

The entertainment is something else.
The band—its rhythm rocks.
The go-go girls are pretty indeed
For longshoremen from the docks.

You can criticize the place all day,
An' really give it heck.
But it's the only place in my hometown
That'll cash my rubber checks.

God and Me

Your troubles abound; they're all around.
Life isn't easy, you see.
But one thing's as sure as I'm standing here:
You can count on God and me.

You work real hard and keep up your guard.
But people can pick with glee.
They say they're a friend, but in the end,
You got only two: God and me.

You've done wrong, we've said all along.
But of guilt, the others aren't free.
I know for sure they're not that pure,
And they don't have God and me.

When you're torn apart, it hurts my heart.
From trouble I want to be free.
We both feel bad when you're so sad,
Your friends—God and me.

When a year goes past, and you have peace at last
Because you're stronger than adversity,
The troubles today will seem far away
From you and God and me.

Green Winter

The winter scene has left me green
With envy for Southern folk.
With the balmy breeze and palmy trees,
I'm sick of winter's jokes.

Even tho from the sault, winter makes me blue.
I'm certainly no Eskimo.
I'd rather sip martinis, watch girls in bikinis
On a beach where the tide does flow.

But for now, I'm trapped and thoroughly crapped
On by ice and drifting snow.
But my day will come, with my place in the sun.
I'll live till to heaven I go.

February 1978

Humility

Did you ever think your crap didn't stink
And you really had it made?
Did you ever feel that in life's deal,
You had finally made the grade?

Well, about that time, when life's sublime
And nothin' can get you down.
Then in one quick blow, life lays you low,
And you're crawlin' around on the ground.

Joys of the Season

Here comes winter and the joys of the season—
Leaves me broke, cold, and lost to reason.
First comes Thanksgiving with lots to eat—
Turkey, cranberries, and a meal complete.
By the time I recover and my tummy's back to size,
Christmas is upon us, before our eyes.
We eat more goodies and much to drink.
By now, our innards are completely on the blink.
And to make it worse, with all the shopping,
My checking account just keeps on dropping.
But cheer up, friend; it's now New Year's Eve.
One more day, and you get a reprieve.
As the night wears on, you decide to change your ways—
Good, sound logic through your alcoholic haze.
It takes two weeks to finally recover,
To rinse out your stomach from all that clutter.
By the middle of March, the bills are all paid.
And just then, you think you've got it made.
Then, when the cold winter finally is nearly done,
Some jerk'll say to you, "Aren't the holidays fun!"

La Mar y Mi Alma

En muchos respectos, mi alma y personalidad,
Son como la mar. Este es un teoriá
Interesante, especialmente desde toda mi
Familia, que eran marineros. No soy un marinero,
Pero un parte de mi alma es.

La mar es Honda y tambien mi alma.
La mar es llena de vida como mi alma.
La mar es fria, y aveces estoy frio.
La mar es caliente, y tengo un parte de
Mi alma que siempre es caliente.
En las estaciones del año, la mar es
Differente, y yo soy differente durante
El ano.
Un persona con un Corazon tiene que
Querer la mar. Y yo espero que
Me quiseriá un persona con un
Corazon.

La vida en tierra empezó en lar mar,
Y tambien la vida de mi familia estaban
En la mar.
A veces yo halló soledad y tranquilidád en

¿La mar. La mar me dió paz. D es possible,
Que yo doy paz a la mar?

Hay sietes mares. Ahora hay solo cinco
Partes de mi cuerpo: yo y los quartos
Ninos. ¿Es possible que hay dos mas partes?
Ydonde?

Yo pienso de mi futuro, y peinso del
Futuro de la mar. ¿Es possible tener
Un alma y la mar por infinidad?

Febrero 1976

La Vida Dulce

Mira, amiga, era un hombre muy, muy libre.

Pero ahora tengo un situacion muy diferente.
Mi vida de un "playboy" estaba algo famosa.
No puedo creer que tengo ahora una esposa.
En vez de las "affairs" muy romantico,
En adición a mi esposa, tengo en otro niño.

Puedes tu creerlo; tenemos un Nuevo muchacho.
En adición a lost otros, me pongo muy nervioso.
Misotros niños, Estevo y hijita Erica,
Simplemente hacen mi vida trágica.

El bebe llora, lost otros gritan, Y mi esposa?
Ella creé que mi dinero es algo para gasta.
La casa esta llena de las cosas del chiquitito,
Mi cerveza caliente, y mi cena esta fria.

Cuando viene la noche y la luna esta llena,
Yo tengo en mi cabeza una idea muy romantica.
Las velas son suaves, y tambien los besos.
Entonces grita el nina; tiene pantalones sucios.

Pero realemente, mi amiga, no quero portarme,
Porque mi vida es major, y este punto lo se.
La cosa es dificil, y hay muchos problemas, pero
No hay importancia, cuando Cathy dice, "Yo te quero."

Leahy's Bluff

Two cold, dark spires against a sky
Of slate-gray clouds, a wind blows by.
Dark gray shingles, worn and rough,
Hide the legend of Leahy's Bluff.

Barely visible as you drive on by,
It's covered with leaves, brown and dry.
What secrets lie within those slopes—
What hates, what loves, what futile hopes?

It sits all soaked in darkened moss.
Its worldly value seems a total loss.
Have those oaken rafters high above
Ever witnessed a human love?

Could it be that many years before,
Happy people passed through that blackened door?
That there were really hopes and dreams,
Long forgotten by decaying beams?

No house breathes by its very own;
It needs human love to be a home.
I wonder if there will ever be enough
To warm again Leahy's Bluff.

Lunch Alone

To pick a bone when I eat lunch alone,
I get so damn depressed.
It's true indeed; I have a need
To have my noontime thoughts expressed.

I either sit on a stool and look like a fool
Or share a solitary table.
If I had my druthers, I'd lunch with others.
I only wish that I were able.

I hope someday after we move away,
I'll work with an amiable group
Who, if they had their druthers, would be with others
When at noon we slurp our soup.

February 1978

Monday, Monday

Well, here it is, a Monday morn.
Why do I feel so damn forlorn?
At the start of another brand-new week,
I crawl out of bed; my bones, they creak.
I think about what I have to do.
No wonder Mondays are always blue.

I kiss my coffee and drink my wife;
I'm out the door, devoid of life,
Crawl into the car and slam the door,
Spill my keys all over the floor.
I'm at my desk still half-asleep.
I pray the Lord my soul to keep.
(He answers me with heavenly scorn,
"I never do that on Monday morn.")

So I plod along and do my thing
And wait for those five bells to ring,
Then return to the comfort of my castle
And try to forget the Monday hassle.
Over a drink, I pause and speak:
"Thank God Monday comes just once a week."

Ode to a Rainstorm

The rain came down like sheets and blankets,
And probably pillows too.
I wondered if it would ever stop
And when it would be through.

Lightning sliced a swath across the sky
Like a great celestial sword.
The thunder roared like a runaway train
Or a very angry Lord.

Slowly, the water began to rise
And lift me from the slab.
I could feel us as we began to float.
My domicile had become my residential boat.

I steered my ark as best I could,
This hulking barge of bricks and wood.
I know someday this rain still stop
And my living ship will land.
I hope it'll be on a desert isle
On a beach of drying sand.

Before dawn, May 30, 2015

On Friends

I've lately come to think a lot
About friends who are real, and those who are not.
Every time you develop a relationship,
This supposed friend gives you the slip.

To get close to a person is impossible,
And to maintain a friendship highly improbable.
I think the best that one can achieve
Is a superficial acquaintance whom you can't believe.

True friends with whom you can share your soul
Don't really exist on the whole.

On Life

Life, it seems, is full of dreams
That break, pop, and shatter.
But if there's a heaven above,
And a world of love,
It really doesn't matter.

What's important to me—and you'll agree—
Is not the parts that go wrong
But the beautiful things that this world brings
As life goes rolling along.

I'll say it out loud: there's no black cloud
That picks on any one person.
But if you want to keep score, and see which is more,
Life is better than worsen.

On Painting

Of all the jobs around the house,
There's one that drives me crazy.
Now remember, I'm not a complaining louse,
And really not that lazy.

But this one task, above all others,
Is one that seems to be
The one I'd skip if I had my druthers;
That's what painting is to me.

I spend a day just scraping walls
In agonizing preparation
For adding color to these hallowed halls—
A panoramic aberration.

Then I place drop cloths with meticulous care
And open my bucket of paint.
Then I cover those walls so utterly bare.
The Sistine Chapel this ain't.

When evening comes and I'm finally through,
I've managed to paint it all.
I've speckled the rug and furniture too,
With even a little on the walls.

September 1977

On Plants

I've written about the friends I know,
The family I love, what life can show.
But of all the scribble I've put into rhyme,
About our plants, I've never penned a line.

You know, plants are folks just like yourself.
They eat and breathe while on the shelf.
They move and grow and communicate
While sitting there so darn sedate.

They do get sick and need some fixin',
From potting soil to Hyponex mixin'.
Their stalks get weak and need support.
Old roots turn gray, some folks report.

They move their leaves to follow the sun.
They close their eyes when the day is done.
They like to be clean, I do believes.
My wife even takes to dusting their leaves.

Plants like good music; they're so darn smart.
They turn off to rock and prefer Mozart.
If you will listen, they'll talk to you.
If you pass nearby, they'll plant a kiss or two.

We need these creatures of the earth.
They're as necessary as childbirth.
They give us oxygen; we give them CO_2—
A partnership formed by God, it's true.

So here's to plants; long may they live
In my humble home—such a joy to give.
Besides, without them, it's true, I say,
We wouldn't need no macramé.

On Rain

Have you ever spent a rainy day
With your thoughts a mile away
And heard each plop of a waterdrop
As you contemplate life's play?

What hopes and dreams do you conjure up
As the rain comes beating down?
You feel confined, yet within your mind
Breathes a freedom without bound.

The weather keeps our bodies in,
But our minds are free to roam.
The dismal gloom fills the quiet room
And compels me to stay at home.

This desolation has a special charm,
One that I know quite well.
When the thunder peals, my body feels
The tug of that awful spell.

When the rain is done and it's dry again,
And I'm free to leave my room,
It seems to be—and you'll have to agree—
That somehow, I prefer the gloom.

Prefootball Cheer

Sunday afternoon is here. Let's have a cheer!
Football games, sandwiches, and beer—
Who will we root for? I really don't care.
Sit by the TV in your big easy chair.

Don't make the kids go play outside.
Keep 'em by the TV; inside hide!
NFL, AFL—really doesn't matter!
Potato chips, cold beer—keep getting fatter.

Alex Karras, Howie Cosell—they're our heroes.
Faces glued to the screen, it's better than front rows.
When is it over? Let's have a cheer!
Professional football now runs all year.

Don't enjoy the outdoors! Don't read books!
Those are the kinda things only for schnooks.
If we fight right and watch real hard,
We can build a nation of illiterate lard.

Rehab—My Little Shop of Horrors

I came back to my room all stiff and sore,
But I knew the work was good for me.
I pause and reflect with aching joints,
Five more hours in my penitentiary.

It seems so long since I slipped and fell
And it turned me upside down
And I began my life as a shattered crip,
And my life a living hell.

My doc was fine, her work divine,
But it was the techs who caused me grief
With their ghoulish grins and gleeful eyes,
With five long hours and no relief.

But as I sit at home, my walker near,
And my joints all stiff and sore,
I muse of my hours under house arrest.
In a twisted way, I miss my shop of horror.

October 2015

Shawn's Back Door

Shawn's Back Door will forevermore
Be a place that's special to me.
The food is hot, the beer is not,
And I had my first date with Mary C.

A Greek named Cris owns all this
With Ellen, his good right hand.
He's kind of cool; he ain't no fool.
Actually, he's a pretty good man.

If you spit on the floor, you're out the door.
This place has got some class.
You make your choice; if you raise your voice,
You're out in the street on your ass.

The music at night ain't no delight.
But what do you want for free?
Ya gotta realize when they harmonize,
This ain't the Grand Ole Opry.

Well, you gotta admit—and this ain't no shit—
That Shawn's is the last of its kind.
And as for me, as you can see,
It's one helluva place to unwind.

Suburbia

Part I—The Suburban Prison

The summer is hot, the sky is blue,
Kids are cranky, fights ensue.
At Little League games, tempers flame.
To live in suburbia—is that your aim?

Neat little houses line up in a row.
Neat little station wagons zip to and fro.
Neat little housewives and their coffee klatches—
Neat little discussions, gossip hatches.

Fathers go to work; some come home.
They say it's business, but they probably roam.
At weekend parties with beer and macaroni
Are the same bored faces, all very phony.

Have 2.2 children, then join the clubs,
Tennis and bridge, and learn to give snubs.
They build their pools with neat precision;
They sit in their houses and watch television.

How they love their kids; about them, they babble
While sipping martinis and playing Scrabble.
But they don't even know the kids they bear.
And when their kids need them, they're never there.

Yes, this is suburbia, lush and green,
Where security lives but is never seen.
By the time you move in, and the sun has risen,
There's no way out of the suburban prison.

Part II—Escape from Prison

Through the night air, bells played a hymn.
Was this the place we were imprisoned in?
Is it really true that once you "arrive,"
You must join in if you want to survive?

No, by God, we'll put up a fight.
We'll escape suburbia this very night.
It won't be easy; we must be quiet.
Our very decision could cause a riot.

We'll try to live as we really should,
Not just to please the neighborhood.
The kind of friends we have will be
The people we really want to see.

We'll avoid the pools, with their assorted fools,
And all the stupid suburban rules.
Forget tennis, bridge, and the community play
And that bigoted clique in the PTA.

And when it comes to ourselves, we'll try to be
Something unheard of: a family.
I'll return to your arms at the end of the day
And not find an excuse just to stay away.

And we can do all this, if we really try.
Only then can we look ourselves in the eye.
And by the time another sun has risen,
We will have escaped the suburban prison.

Tarde

Yo quieró escribir un poema
De mi favorita tema
De la esposa que yo quiero.
Para ti, siempre espero.

Porqúe esta ella muy despacio,
Cuando estoy muy, muy rapido?
Ésta es todo mi cuento
De la mujere que yo encueñtro.

The Ballad of Mohawk Mike

Prologue

They told this tale many years ago.
I don't know if it's true; some say it's so.
It tells of a special breed of men
Who work high steel as no one can.

⁓

This is the ballad of Mohawk Mike,
Who came down from Canada on the iron pike.
They say he left after killing a man
In a barroom brawl over a girl named Ann.
I don't know if it's true; I really don't care.
He was a helluva man who worked in the air.

He worked as a shaker and bolter too,
Then moved right up to a connectin' crew.
No preacher was he; he was as hard as a nail—
Didn't take no lip from man nor quail.
He worked all day an' drank all night.
That man of steel, God, he could fight.

I first met Mike on the Narrows Bridge.
We were connectin' iron on that spindly ridge.
In all the years that I'd worked high steel,
I never knew a man who had his feel.
He handled the iron as a groom, his bride
As patient as hell and with a touch of pride.

Well, we got to be real good drinkin' chums,
From dark to dawn in Gotham's slums,
Together shared the ladies of the night,
Were back-to-back in many a fight.
But when morning came an' the whistle blew,
There was Mike, first in his crew.

We had worked together a year or so,
And then one day when things were slow,
Mike said to me in a casual way,
"Ya know, my friend, I got to say,
If I ever had to depend on a man,
I could depend on you; by God, I can."

We were finishing up a job that fall,
A simple frame sixty stories tall.
Things had gone along as smooth as hell.
The iron all fit like nuts in a shell.
We were settin' steel at a floor a day.
For better than a month, it had gone this way.

We jumped the crane at forty-four,
Set all the steel, then called for more,
Tier by tier, reachin' up for the top,
Six more floors, and then we could stop.
The last columns were up without a fuss
And just made the chord of a wind-bent truss.

An' then it happened, I don't know how.
A spandrel abeam took one helluva wow.
Mike called for the crane, and strung up a hitch
And hollered, "I'll straighten that son of a bitch."
He scaled a column to the very top
Fifty-eight floors up—one helluva drop.

Mike hollered at me, "Hold that line!"
Sweat rolled in my eyes; I could taste that brine.
I knew we had drank too much that day.
My mind was fogged; I started to sway.
But I held that line, just as tight as hell.
I wouldn't be blamed if someone fell.

He pulled the pins that held the joint,
A hundred eyes on that eagle's point.
Then a broken line whipped like a thread.
An Indian scream—Christ, Mike was dead.
God, that wail hung in my ears.
My face was soaked in a sheet of tears.

There wasn't much left of that Indian brave
Fifty-eight floors below in a muddy grave.
But we buried Mike with a funeral fittin'
For a man as cold as steel, lean, hard-bitten'.
And he lies today six feet below
A column baseplate, on E prime row.

I left the business; I was done as hell.
I'd lost my nerve, just an empty shell.
I went into sales over on Fifty-Seventh Street,
Earned enough to drink and enough to eat.
And whenever I see a bloodred frame,
Mike and I know I was to blame.

—————

Epilogue
They say a building must take a life
An' leave small children a wailing wife.
Ironworkers are a superstitious lot.
Some folks are, and some are not.
But an ironworker knows, or so they say,
When his number is up and it's his judgment day.

The Bell Will Toll Twenty-Nine Times

Prologue

Three years have passed since she was seen last
By a soul who's living still,
And it seems to me to be an eternity
Since I was told this tale I tell.

———〜———

It was in a saloon off a Lake Erie lagoon
That I met this strange old man.
He had a beard of white, eyes as dark as night.
His skin was white and showed every light.
No colder could my blood have become.
They held me so I couldn't have run.

In a chilly word, he said, "I'm Ed Fitz,
And I own this wayside tavern.
And if you'd care for an ale, I'll tell ya a tale
That will make your stomach turn."

I pulled up a stool and listened to this ghoul
Tell a story about a November blitz,
About twenty-nine men who were never seen again,
And a ship they called the *Fitz*.

"You heard the belief she was sunk on a reef
By a storm that blew straight out of hell.
You also heard that she went to her grave
When a forty-foot wave on her fell.

"Well, I swear to you none of it's true.
No living man knows her fate.
On that storied sea in the devil's wake,
I know the truth on the roiling lake.

"The price man pays for using the devil's lake
Is to exact a toll of ships and men.
No matter how big and stout they be,
The fate of a ship was to be a mystery.

"Later, a bigger and better one came off the ways.
The spirit of the lake took this ship, the *Fitz*.
But because of the evil of that one,
Twenty-nine men will not rest till justice is done.

"They will float unseen by any means
Till justice is finally done.
And each of our souls will rest
When their reward is finally won."

The Demise

I sit here, in this quiet office,
And wish it were a bit more raucous.
I look on this dreary scene
And long for pastures much more green.

What happened in the last six years
That made us get far in arrears?
Was it something we did really so wrong,
Or did we not sell ourselves all along?

Was R. C. R. somewhat to blame?
He was a greedy man; he had no shame.
He got his money and kept us broke.
I'm sure he enjoys his little joke.

Vance and Virginia got their share.
And now we're broke! Is it really fair?
That benevolent despot "Uncle Ray"
Still robs us today through Virginia's pay.

Enough of blaming the other guy.
Our plans just went completely awry.
We're not businessmen, I must admit.
I wish others could face up to it.

As I look around this tomb-like room,
I see dozing people, impending doom.
I must leave this dying place
So I can still look at me in the face.

Life's too short to pass my time
With nothing to do, without a dime.
I'll admit that I made a big mistake.
That fact is not too hard to take.

And what do I do, and where do I go?
At this point in time, I really don't know.
But I do know that God won't let me down.
I'm ready today—a future abounds.

January 1977

The Doings of a Drone Named Dum

Dum flew so high on a sunny sky,
Reaching heights a mile high.
He felt the wind beneath his rotor,
As if propelled by a celestial motor.

And when the signal came to fly on home,
Dum felt crushed, sad, so very alone.
He longed to fly across the space.
He likened himself to a World War One ace.

Then one day, he said, "I'll fly away,
And I won't return at the end of the day."
The world at last would be his only chart,
"If only I could have a heart."

When that day came, he revved on the pad
And flew for himself with all he had.
You may see him in a distant sky
Among the cirri a mile high.

Epilogue

So to a different beat, he beat his drum.
It's plain to see this drone's not dumb.

Before dawn, February 20, 2017

The Family Doctor

How many times do you sit and wait
For the family doctor, who's always late?
You rush to get to your appointment on time
Just to sit and wait at the end of the line.

You sit in a room with hard-back chairs.
Time drags on, and nobody cares.
There's only one magazine in this sterile room:
A 1966 copy of *Bride and Groom*.

In the examining room, you're finally seated—
Ah, your long, long wait nearly completed.
The nurse says with a smile to you,
"The doctor will be in, in a second or two."

Minutes turn to hours; time rushes by.
It's not from disease but of old age you'll die.
Did you ever kill time in an examining room?
Those chalk-white walls cast a sterile gloom.

You read the labels on all his jars,
Take your blood pressure, hit the tuning bars.
Count the cotton balls and tongue depressors too.
Kleenex—six boxes. Sterile swabs—102.

About that time, you're ready to go berserk.
In he walks with a silly smirk.
"Sorry, your disease isn't on my list.
I'll have to send you to a specialist."

The Great Hoax

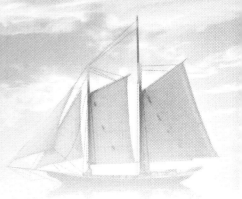

This energy crunch is a great big bunch
Of garbage, I really think.
It isn't fair the way they scare
And push us past the brink.

They feed us lies, yet before our eyes,
They waste and squander and spend.
They close the schools and behave like fools.
When will all this end?

To be a priority, you pay a royalty
To the proper high official.
Then they take the fuel from the same grade school.
Now isn't that judicial?

There's nothing ranker than to sink a tanker
And litter the coast with oil.
Then they say, "Higher prices you'll pay."
It makes my blood really boil.

Leave industry in a lurch, and close a church
While liquor stores stay wide open.
They open the mall; arenas play ball.
Things'll change, I'm really hopin'.

The whole thing's a hoax, just one of their jokes
To strangle and take control.
But the thing they forget is the American wit.
Screw the gas; we'll heat with coal.

February 1977

The Creeping Shadow

I want to write about the plight
Of a struggling engineer.
He's sort of cool and ain't no fool
But frustrated as hell, I fear.

The work is neat, it can't be beat,
And the money's not too bad.
But the thing that's tough and makes life rough
Is a partner who makes him mad.

This can't be chose; that's the way it goes.
But God, does he have to act
With all the class of a horse's ass
And lack a thing called *tact*?

It's bad enough that he's so gruff
With the people who work for him.
But it's sad I feel when he acts like a heel
With the clients who feed our kin.

There're times, by God, ya could hit the clod,
But that wouldn't help, I'm sure.
Please don't take offense, but he's so dense.
With his hands, he couldn't find his rear.

Now, don't complain. It taxes your brain
And makes your blood pressure higher.
Try to remember it won't last forever;
It'll quit the minute you retire.

The Little People, East of Eden

Is it right to have to live in fear
From those so cruel for so many years?
Why can't they simply leave us alone
And never wire, write, or phone?
Haven't they done enough to this person?
Must they make the situation worsen?
They nearly destroyed a beautiful life
Of a decent person who is now my wife.
They tried to kill her, and her child too,
Mostly mentally but physically too.
And even tho she's moved away,
This haunting ghost continues to prey.

I think they're really scared as hell.
They love only greed and evil too well.
I've never seen a man quite so small
Who cheats and lies into his own selfish wall,
And a woman so sick of mind and heart
She's afraid her world will fall apart.
As I see it, there are two weak links,
And these will cause their world to sink.
This spineless woman will finally crack.
And that faithless man with no bone in his back

Will sink in his quagmire of lies and deceit,
And then God's justice will finally be complete.

Those two souls that they tried to kill
Will grow in faith and will love instill
In another family that really needs them,
Not too unlike the family of Bethlehem.
It's not that they'll never have any trouble,
But they'll never fall into that lying rubble.
And this woman whose life I clasp
Will start a family that has no past.
We'll grow in faith and in God's heavenly swell
While East of Eden will sink into eternal hell.

The Mind

The mind is a funny kind of thing;
Such joy, such pain that mass can bring.
It makes you dull, makes you think,
Relaxes your bod, pushes you to the brink.

When you reach this point and you think you're crazy,
It'll change its tact and make you lazy.

When I try to remember some important fact,
It leaves me stranded—a complete lack of tact.
But something bad that I'd just as soon forget
Stays with me; the thought won't split.

It grows with me, helps educate.
Its moral fiber helps me to the pearly gate.
It makes me smart so I can find a job,
Then with a fickle turn makes me a worthless slob.

But let's face it; your mind's with you
From your conception till the day you shoot through.
And I guess if I really had my druthers,
I'd keep my mind above all others.

October 1977

The Sea

The ocean roared; its anger soared.
As the sea-foam got high in the sky
With quickened pace, it seared my face.
With its wrath, how many soon would die?

The ships I saw leaned to their yawls,
As hell-bent as nature's foe,
So large, abeam, yet how small they seemed
As they were tossed about, to and fro.

Will sailors die? Will children cry
As God's torrent surges ashore?
Will the seawall fall and cover all,
To be buried forevermore?

But then for some unknown reason, not like this tropic season,
This wrath steered away
And spared for now; yes, God did allow
But would return another day.

August 1985

Una Oracion

Dios mio, porque estoy aqui
Cuando prefiero estar alli
Con mi esposa y familia
En mi casa muy sencilla
Y el sol sobre mi cabeza
Con una botella de cerveza
En el patio con mi silla
Con una bebida muy, muy fria?
¿Porque no estar doude prefiero?
Porque necesito mas dinero!
Y está, mi querida, Ivi.
Es una poema para ti, vi.

Waterville

A town so quaint with folks who ain't,
And that typical suburban flair,
People gossip a lot; nice they're not.
Their warmth can chill the air.

When we moved to town, word got around
That we weren't their stereotype.
So we were barred from the club and given the snub.
My god, the smell was ripe.

To be truly fair, I really don't care
We're not their usual kind.
If they just let us be and not crucify,
The family and I don't mind.

The neighbors on either side had never lied;
They said the town had many faces.
I wonder if they realized that before their eyes
Was one of those Peyton Places.

When to Waterville we came, it wasn't our aim
To buy the whole damn town.
We bought a home, and we'll live alone,
And they're not gonna get me down.

We'll keep our noses clean,
Enjoy the cool's friends in between
To ignore those folks and their suburban jokes.
We'll end up happier than those yokes.

January 1978

White Birch Lodge

White Birch Lodge: a place to be
To live with nature in harmony.
The food is great, the water fine.
The sailing's cool, the beach divine.

A staff superb, eager, and rarin'
With Cliff, Ruby, Rick, and Karen,
The rest of the group is also neat.
Craze and Sav make our day complete.

Our waitress, Marcia, waits on our table.
At serving food, she's quite able.
It fills our wives' more frequent wishes
Not to cook the food nor do the dishes.

Captain Al, with his sailing ship,
Gives us a thrill and one heckuva trip.
The softball games leave our muscles sore.
But the very next night, we're back for more.

As I sit on the beach, the waves're a-lappin',
The moon overhead, the fire crackin'.
When it comes to Saturday and away we file,
Our week up here makes the year worthwhile.

Winter '78

It's plain to see this weather's obscene
And the whole damn winter stinks.
It's as cold as hell, and you can't stay well
Without a couple of drinks.

This cursed cold has got hold
And chilled me to the bone.
I'm damn near done, and not the only one;
In misery, I'm not alone.

When the power went out, I was about to shout
And rant, scream, and swear.
But the words, they froze when they left my nose.
So you'll hear 'em when spring thaws the air.

February 1978

Friends I Have Known and Loved

A Fisher of Men

There is a man; his name is Ray.
He serves our Lord most every day.
He's not your average kind of priest.
He's got the couth of a savage beast.

Despite his class (he's kind of crass),
He does his job; he says the Mass,
Works at his desk day by day.
He doesn't complain; I guess that's Ray.

But this here man is something rare.
When you need his help, he's always there.
When I was sick, he came along.
When I was weak, he made me strong.

And these words fit another man
Who was here when our faith began.
And you can smile when this I say:
Fisher is the Christ who's alive today.

Circa 1967

An Ode to Sue

The time has come, old Sue, my chum,
To talk about your years.
I suppose I'm bold to say you are so old,
But then reticence is not one of my fears.

They say the brain is the first to wane,
And I believe that's probably true,
'Cause with the things you forget keeping me continually upset,
I know it has happened to you.

You forget their raises, go through surly phases,
And yet don't ever seem upset.
You misfile the mail, misspell without fail,
And completely confuse your president.

But you know, my dear, something is clear:
Our friendship is a healing salve.
So though you may be feeble, you're one of my favorite people.
You're the best Tonto a kemosabe could ever have.

Ivi

Ivi, tu eres mi amiga favorita,
Una Diosa Griega muy bonita,
Una profesora sin equalidad,
Una persona hermosa de qualidad.

Jess Mills

The time has come, Jess, my chum,
To pen a line or two.
The truth must be told; you're growing old.
As a young man, you're totally through.

You may scoff at me and say, "Wait and see.
I'm as virile as ever before."
But according to complaints from your conjugal mate,
You don't get it up anymore.

Your appendectomy was an example, you see,
Of the way that aging starts.
A zipper was installed when you were overhauled
To facilitate replacement of parts.

But don't feel sad; it ain't that bad,
'Cause age has certain graces,
'Cause to tell the truth and with the problems of youth,
Neither of us would ever trade places.

Marika

Of all the gals who are my pals,
You're really one of a kind,
Strong on looks and good with the books,
Blessed with a brilliant mind.

You have the ambition and the intuition
To be a great engineer.
When you take your test, you'll pass with the best;
Of this I have no fear.

You're lucky indeed to have the man you need.
You complement each other so much.
You're an interesting pair, with an intellectual flair.
And it's amazing you're not even Dutch.

February 1978

Marlene and Joe

Marlene and Joe, on the go—
When will they ever stop?
They're always here, always there.
If it was me, I think I'd drop.

Joe teaches; his fiddle screeches.
When will he ever slow down?
When he has the urge, he writes a dirge.
And his music goes 'round and 'round.

Marlene teaches; her talent reaches
To fields both near and far.
At church, she's heard, reading the Word
Or strumming her Spanish guitar.

But when it comes to friends, my chums,
They're a pair that can't be beat.
And so I say this very day,
Those two are really neat.

Mi Amiga

Ã mi amiga, que favorita.
Yo tengo esta bebida
A tu salud, y tu menud.
Y tu cara es muy bonita.

Ode to Holly

Pickin' teeth ain't beneath
The tech by the name of Holly.
And in the chair, she has a flair
With a drill; she's kind of handy.

She cleans the crud with a silver spud
And sweeps the germs away.
And when she flosses, the pain's colossus.
How can she do it all day?

The doc is fine, his works divine.
But our favorite is quite plain.
And if she could, I know she would
Eliminate all dental pain.

February 2014

Ode to Jan

The time has come, my therapist chum,
To write a little poem.
It seems to me when we're in therapy,
You make us feel at home.

Your approach is divine as you delve into my mind.
You're thorough and don't miss a blink.
When compared to your peers, one has little fears
That you're really one helluva shrink.

Now, me, I concede, ain't easy indeed
To get to know what I'm feelin'.
I'm quick with my wit, and a little full of shit.
It ain't with no ordinary dummy you're dealin'.

But if I know you, you'll eventually get through
And find out what's inside this dome.
You'll have me showing my feelings and send my emotions
reeling.
Thanks, Jan, for helping make a happy home!

December 1981

Ode to Marty

When it comes to a shrink, I really think
You're probably the top of the heap.
In your therapeutic role, you soothe my soul
And help with a good night's sleep.

At times, you make me mad or even sad
'Cause I never know what will follow.
I get so vexed and even perplexed,
As into my psyche I wallow.

But the "bottom line," as you say so fine,
Is not pain of therapy
But the feeling I get when I dump my shit
And make my life work for me.

April 1983

Paul and the Holy Spirits

I want to take some time to pen a little rhyme
About your musical group.
It added class, with a touch of brass.
Our thanks to your minstrel troop.

It was really swell; they played so well.
Even our kids were listening.
You had inspiration and great intonation
From those silver trumpets glistening.

How sad it'd be, and I think you'd agree,
If there was no music in the Mass.
And when we die and attend Mass in the sky,
They'll have a folk group, with brass.

Please give my best to all the rest,
And thanks from all our parish.
But above it all, it was good to see you, Paul,
In a Mass we'll always cherish.

March 1977

The Boss

Prologue

I was sittin' in the dooley one day.
My thoughts were miles away
When this little rhyme
Popped into my mind.
It was something I had to say.

———∽———

St. Joe's Church would be in a lurch.
Our faith would take a loss
If we didn't have that anointing salve—
A priest we call "the Boss."

Well, the Boss came in when we needed him
To get us off our duff
With a man named Ray; they saved the day
And made Satan's work more tough.

It wasn't fun to get things done.
People were hard to please.
It seemed to me an eternity
To end communion on our knees.

Committees conceived, the establishment grieved,
The voice of the people heard.
There's more to church than in a pulpit perch
And saying God's Holy Word.

When the going's rough, and they're giving him guff,
He gets up and eloquently speaks:
"Don't blame me; why can't you see
I've only been here a coupla weeks?"

The Mastery of Joe

You've finally mastered the fiddle?
Or is it something else in the middle?
Has your fiddling around been mastered?
Or is the master fiddler plastered?

After all this time, it's good to see
That you've developed your skill to a new degree
And that your working and fretting is through
And you've reached an accord with BGSU.

I suppose Maumee will keep you on the staff
And won't give you any more gaff
Now that you're really a teacher of note.
Too bad that bond issue didn't float!

But now, to get serious for a time:
If you'll forget the flats in my sharp rhyme,
I'll say before I let my poetry worsen,
You really are one helluva person.

The Time of Sheri

A wife died; the family cried.
The husband tried; his hands were tied.
He had his grief, but that was brief.
To keep belief, he craved relief.

Some tried to do, but they left too.
And then you came to ease a pain.
You gave of yourself; you gave a wealth
Of love and joy to a girl and boy.

The world revolved; you got involved,
Washed the clothes, and cooked the meals—
From Maumee to Monclova wore out your wheels,
Always around, never let them down.

You helped a man know life again,
Gave him hope, straightened out the dope.
From you, he learned that love is earned—
Because of this, found what he missed.

Time passed away till at last one day,
The time had come; your job was done.
A wife has arrived, new life has thrived,
But because of you, he made it through.

1976

To Budd and Val

The time has come, Budd, my chum,
To pen a line or two.
To your marital pal, our friend, Val,
This poem is for the both of you.

It's a pity, for all's sake, we usually take
Folks like you for granted.
But friends like you—and this is true—
Grow like seeds when planted.

An' speaking of seeds, among the weeds,
Our three kids really love you.
No angels by far, but whose kids are?
They're the reason we live as we do.

Who else but Val is the kind of pal
Who can face us on Monday morn?
She cleans the house as quick as a mouse
And puts up with all my corn.

I know you're wishin' you could be fishin'
When you take the kids to town.
But you're the kinda guy—and this ain't no lie—
Who just can't let folks down.

As this poem ends, my dearest friends,
Remember a thing or two.
Cathy and me, we both agree
You're real friends tried and true.

To Joe on the Big 5-0

Tonight, we're here to talk about
The deeds of this rather boorish lout.
You've heard me give him bounteous praises
In more precise and eloquent phrases.

Yes, this here man, rather old and wrinkled,
Whose musical talents are sparsely sprinkled—
He is the reason we're here tonight
And missing the NFL weekly delight.

But we don't mind this inconvenience.
Besides, there's no place to air our grievance.
Of course, if I really had my druthers,
It's obvious I'd rather be with others.

But dear old Joe, don't be dismayed.
Don't let your nerves get tattered and frayed.
Remember tonight, as you view with chagrin,
You'll never be fifty years old again.

December 1978

To Sandy

You type the letters and clean the place.
We depend on you for a smiling face.
And until we nearly let you go,
I never realized that this is so.

You take care of all sorts of things,
Answer the phone every time it rings,
And boil our coffee to keep us awake,
And think of all the flak you take.

And my lady, you've been a good friend.
How many times your ear did I bend?
You're the kind of steno that's rare indeed.
Your work is excellent; we're all agreed.

And so, my Sandy, when you're feeling low,
There's something important that you should know.
You're as fine a person as we've had in this place
And one helluva asset to the human race.

1975

Animals I Have Known
and Mostly Loved

A Feisty Day

Feisty Bear has a flare
For getting in heaps of trouble.
With lack of tact, she has a knack
For making me see double.

I want to say that just today,
Here are some of the things she's done:
Spilled milk on the floor, caught Beau in the door,
And thought that was really fun.

She bit Fruta's ear, spilled my beer,
And put a frog in Emmy's chicken soup,
Pulled Faceus's tail, lost the mail,
And tracked in all Beau's poop.

She let Steve's mice out, scattered the litter about,
And flushed Legos down the toilet bowl
And put a tear in the piano-room chair.
Her havoc has taken its toll.

But what's so sad, if you think that's bad,
Is then I'm doing you no favor
When I have to say that as for today,
Feisty was on pretty good behavior.

June 1984

Charlie Chip

My Charlie Chip is quite a pip,
That little old dog of mine.
He chews on his bone when left alone;
It's his most favorite way to dine.

He scatters his toys, like all little boys,
And never picks up a thing,
'Cause Gramps will come, clean every one
So he doesn't end up in a sling!

When I sit down to read, what I really need
Is my dog to lie by my side.
As I flip through the pages, I'd bet my wages
He knows every last word that's inside.

Now, Sandy has Piggy; she's really a biggie
And will protect her from every harm.
But when harm comes to my door, he's right on the floor,
With his yapping to sound the alarm.

February 2017

Clarence

Every morning, he's always there,
Rain or shine or the searing glare.
He comes to spend a moment or two
To share with me the morning dew.
A silent thought for a brand-new day,
Then just as quickly, he goes away.

In those fleeting moments, we share so much.
We are to each other an invisible crutch.
Just think if all mankind could communicate
As I can with this special primate.
Ya see, my friend Clarence, about whom I care,
Is not a man but an ordinary hare.

August 1977

Santa Moose

There was a moose, a tiny moose,
No bigger than a minute.
Santa's the name, decoration the game,
That pretty little idjit.

He graced the table at Christmastime
In a giant, elegant sleigh.
He gave us joy, that rodent boy,
And took not one cent in pay.

As the season changed, he was rearranged
And plopped in a druggist's jar.
Garnished with straw and flowers tall,
He can be seen from near and far.

Yes, that Santa moose, silly goose,
Gives my wife such joy.
And then the next season, for no darn reason,
She'll make something else from that boy.

February 1977

The Feisty Bear

He came from Germany on Lufthansa Air,
That fuzz ball known as Feisty Bear.
When we brought him in and gave him shelter,
I didn't realize he'd create such helter-skelter.

The spoiled little bear with the surly disposition
Had all of a sudden become a real imposition.
He screamed for his porridge first thing in the morn
With the sweet, dulcet tone of a diesel horn.

And to make matters worse and muddy the air,
He sent to Germany for additional bear
Fratata, Fragita, and Fausta at first,
Followed by Fraulein and Fruta, to make matters worse.

Life at our house will never be the same
Since from the Vaterland six bears came.
With those teutonic terrors with the impish grins,
Our lives will never be the same again!

March 1984

The Saga of Pepé the Puppy

I sat in my house so very alone,
Lapped up my water, and chewed up my bone.
I'm much too bored to sleep anymore,
So all I can do is pace the floor.

And from my window, I saw faraway lands.
Oh, how I yearned to see them firsthand.
Then, one day, they let me out on my own,
Free to romp and free to roam.

I raced across roads and onto the green
And experienced a world I had never seen.
I was in a new world and free to roam,
And I was scared and longed for my very own home.

I retraced my steps on the same gray street
Surrounded with cars nipping at my feet.
The fear I felt for my own little life—
These cars could cut me like steaks to a knife.

Then a kind lady stopped and picked me up.
Then a worried old man helped save this pup.
They guided me through the highway above
And brought me home to those I love.

My mama cried as I leaped to her breast,
And my papí cried, as did the rest—
The kind lady too, as did the old man.
I was sad, for I wouldn't see them again.

Written by Pepé the puppy (with help from my old friend
Gary)

March 2016

The Crusty Crustaceans

The Overture to "The Crabs"

The poems that you are about to read
Are of some folks so strange indeed—
About a breed of life so rare
That can't be believed unless you're there.

The folks this poet is talking about
Are so strange that this tale you'll doubt.
About creatures living in harmony,
This is the story of the crab colony.

You won't believe it, but it's really true;
Crabs live in groups like me and you.
They're born, they die, and do a lot in between.
They work, they play, and are sometimes mean.

Crabs get married and do have families—
Usually, three litters that are called *cribbies*.
They're a happy lot, and carefree too.
Bachelor crabs have an affair or two.

At their jobs, they earn a shell or two
To buy them shrimp and oyster stew.
They like to play and are often seen
In a crabby disco or watching the screen.

I am personally acquainted with several crabs.
I share their joys, and heartfelt stabs.
Many a time, I've worked far into the night
To drag an eight-legged crab from a barroom fight.

No, they're not all rogues or a scurry bunch.
Nose-Pincher and his wife are as nice as punch.
Then there's J. C. Crab and his brand-new bride;
Stella's her name, and she beams with pride.

Well, I've tried to sum it up in one nutshell
About the crabs that I know so well.
How much happiness they've given my wife and I;
We've shared their joy, and with them, we cry.

They're impish dudes as they crawl about,
Looking for a nose to pinch or a tail to tout.
They're silly folks, on brains not too tall.
But one thing's certain: they sure have a ball.

And one more thing that's beautiful too:
No matter where you live or are moving to,
If you really love them, as we surely do,
They'll pack up the whole colony and move with you.

Enough of this dribble and endless rhyme;
It's time to meet these friends of mine.
So relax and read the following verses
Of the story of crabs, for betters or worses.

January 1977

A Postlude of Crabs

An Adult Anthology on a Crab Ecology

Now, you know the crab, that dear little fellow,
They can make you angry, sad, and often mellow.
And if you're lucky, some one of these years,
You might have your own colony of crustacean dears.

January 1976

The New Year's Crab

The New Year's Crab with hat and horn,
Proclaiming the year about to be born,
Drinks and dances the whole night through,
Kissing the pretty lady crabs too.
And when the New Year and day do break,
He has one crabacious headache.

December 1977

The Winter Crab

The Winter Crab, when the weather's cold,
Likes to grab and take hold.
He snuggles in bed and covers his head
And then looks forward to getting bred.

The Winter Crab, with his beady eyes,
Rolls on his back and gets a rise.
Sexy crustacean, his performance dazzles.
When comes the spring, he's worn to frazzles.

The Snow Crab

The Snow Crab bundles up against the storm,
Hell-bent on staying nice and warm.
He's covered with snow from claw to shell,
Trudging along through this icy hell.

He's bundled in fur and a parka too—
On each little claw has a tiny snowshoe.
God, how he'd like to lay on the beach
Far from winter and its icy reach.

Even the Snow Crab is not at home
At −15 Celsius and chilled to the bone.
But the Snow Crab accepts his heavenly fate—
Better than being dinner on someone's plate.

January 1978

The Marriage of Tippy and Chicano

Tippy and Chicano, the nuptial crabs,
Tied the knot the other day.
With bells and rings and lacy things,
Together, they start on life's way.

In a four-ring ceremony with lots of rice,
The groom was so nervous he answered twice.
Stella, she cried, and Harry was shaky,
Esmeralda tearful, Mrs. Nose-Pincher flaky.

A beautiful couple came down the aisle.
Tippy looked cute; Chicano had a smile.
They stood in line and shook all the claws.
The crabs kissed Tippy amid the guffaws.

At a noisy reception at the colony hall,
Lots to eat and drink, they both had a ball.
And we heard them exclaim as they took their flight,
"Thank you all! We'll have a good night."

January 1978

The Valentine Crab

The Valentine Crab, his love he'll grab
With all his eight tiny legs.
To be real dandy, he'll give her candy
In hopes of fertilizing her eggs.

For his heart's completion, this love crustacean
Pops the question of all time.
Please don't this blab, my loving crab.
Will you be my valentine?

February 1977

Linguia Crabia

The Story of How Crabs Blab

Have you ever speculated on how crabs communicate
And the language they use with each other?
Well, they have a tongue unknown to anyone
Except those who love them like a brother.

The verbs are complex; your tongue, it wrecks
As you try to utter their sounds.
They have a collection of nouns and a vocab quite profound.
And a literature really rich abounds.

I learned their speech lying on the beach
And listening to stories grand.
When the truth is known, their culture is overblown;
You take their speech with a grain of sand.

February 1977

The Leprecrab

I've heard it said on Saint Patty's Day,
'Tis the Leprecrabs that romp and play,
Those tiny green crabs from the Emerald Isle
With eight lil shillelaghs to the devil to rile.

Many people don't believe that they exist.
And despite the truth, those rumors persist.
But on March 17, with a greeny sprig,
You'll find them dancing an Irish jig.

They drink Irish whiskey and fight a bit
And sing Gaelic songs, that silly twit.
And ye'll be seven years safe from the devil's grab
If ye truly believe in the Leprecrab.

March 1977

The Springtime Crab

The Springtime Crab spends his day
With a pleasant, delightful roll in the hay.
He likes to lay and warm in the sun.
In spring, he'll have sex with just about anyone.

The Springtime Crab, a playful guy,
Bounds and leaps from ground to sky.
He likes to wrap his legs around you—
All eight of 'em too; that's what he do.

The Engineer Crab

The Engineer Crab, in his technical gab,
Has a keen mathematical mind.
The stresses and strain flow from his brain.
No smarter crab can you find.

His beady eyes gleam as he designs a beam.
His calculator clacks away.
A pencil in each claw, he really can draw.
He's surely well worth his pay.

There's just one quirk in his structural work
And the building his designs provide:
Being crustacean in mind, you'll usually find
The steel skeleton on the outside.

February 1978

Chef Harry

An artisan career of ability unclear,
The food biz came out of the blue.
Harry's the name, and food's the game,
Open for dinners and lunches too.

You're greeted at the door, escorted across the floor
By a crab with a black bow tie.
This little fellow is sometimes less than mellow.
His humor is kind of wry.

But the food is fine and service divine;
That's why I'm writing this ballad.
And the advice I give is "You've never lived
Till you've tried our Harry's salad."

March 1978

Dirty Harry

Dirty Harry, the grubby crab,
Courses with grim, so dark and drab.
He does all the dirty jobs in the colony.
Shunned by the others, he lives lonely.

Dirty Harry, no girl has he
Since he never showers; he's too darn stinky.
He lives downwind of all the others,
But would he live there if he had his druthers?

I really think we could help this dear
And make him accepted by his peers.
He has a sense of humor; he's kind of smart,
Even if he does smell much like a fart.

We'll sneak him into a spraying shower.
In no time at all, he'll smell like a flower.
We'll find him a girl to go out on a date.
Next thing you'll know, he'll be marriage bait.

He'll have cribbies crawling all over his home—
No more to wander, no more to roam.
With all these problems,
I wonder if Dirty Harry really wants to be clean.

March 1977

The Moving Crabs

The crabs were in an uproar.
Confusion reigned supreme.
Governing crabs took to the floor
To discuss their moving scheme.

"Will they take us with them?"
"Can the colony move up north?"
The clatter of shells caused mayhem.
Little claws paced back and forth.

Even the cribbies were confused.
They wondered where to go.
They wondered if they'd be abused,
Left to face the cold and the snow.

They came to us with a delegation
Of serious, very concerned crabs.
They had to discuss the situation,
Which seemed to them quite drab.

We assured these shelled emissaries
That no move would be complete
Without these proper dignitaries,
The colony, all 3,800 feet.

So once again, peace finally reigned.
And the crabs were all excited
That since it had been simply explained,
They would be invited.

March 1977

Nose-Pincher Crab

Nose-Pincher Crab is a mischievous fellow.
When he pinches your nose, you let out a bellow.
Kinda cute tho, ya gotta admit,
If he wasn't such a grabby twit.

Nose-Pincher Crab, sneaky little elf—
If only he'd keep his claws to himself.
Ya gotta suppose when he grabs your nose,
It's really just one of life's nose blows.

The Vacation Crab

The Vacation Crab sits by the ocean,
Soaking up sun and suntan lotion.
He watches the waves crash on the beach
But carefully stays just beyond their reach.

The Vacation Crab, with one eye open,
For some crab flesh he's sort of hopin'.
He keeps his parts covered so they don't get fried—
Not much action when they're shriveled and dried.

May 1977

The Mexican Crabs

The Mexican Crabs, with their colorful shells—
Latin crustaceans, those taco belles—
They don't work hard or take life serious.
Their casual air makes us workers furious.

But the Mexican Crabs are a happy lot.
They love everyone and never get upset.
When you ask 'em to do somethin' they don't wanna,
They clack away and say, "Maybe mañana."

May 1978

The Birthday Crab

The Birthday Crab is really smitten
With his birthday gift, so nice and fittin':
A poop mobile with four on the floor.
The overjoyed crab couldn't ask for more.

The Birthday Crab, when he blows out his candle,
It's almost more than he can handle,
So sing "Happy Birthday," and shake his claw.
"Happy birthday, Crab. Please have a ball."

June 1977

El Chicano Crab

The Chicano Crab es un hombre muy bueno,
Un poco mal, pero tambien sueno.
Este picano, que un chiste,
Dicifil por claro, y differente.

El Chicano Crab, como esta,
Cuidado amigo, con muchos "claws,"
Este crab, que prescosa
Con un persondidad fabuloso?

El suela moviendo es muy intelligente.
Un amigado _____ es la verdad.
Pardios me, que un gran crab.

Junio 1978

A Summer Crab

A summer crab reached out to grab
A sexy boob that did protrude.
And before he could say, "Lobster stew,"
He ended up in bed, and one helluva screw!

The CB Crab

The CB Crab, well, don't you know,
Is frequently heard on the air.
Ya give him a break, and within a shake,
He'll have the twenty on any bear.

"Breaker 1/9 for the crustacean divine."
Ya got him; now, kick it back.
"Hey, good buddy, with claws so muddy,
How's it lookin' over your tracks?"

"Well, it's clean and green—no bears to be seen.
Do it to it on this super slab."
So he puts the pedal to the metal.
That's him: our eighteen-clawed crab.

August 1977

The Pegasus Crab

If in the classics you dab,
There's the Pegasus Crab,
Well known in ancient histories.
When he's tired of the ocean,
He puts his wings in motion
And soars over the tops of the trees.

August 1977

The Autumn Crab

The Autumn Crab, when the weather's drab,
Drags himself about.
He likes to play most all the day
In bed without coming out.

The Autumn Crab, he tries to grab
What he can before the snow
Comes tumbling down to cover the ground
And freezes his parts that show.

The Astronaut Crab

The Astronaut Crab spaces out, pilots,
Circles the globe in the heavenly quiet.
When he splashes down in the familiar ocean,
He's equally at home with that rolling motion.

You saw him on TV leaping across the moon,
Gathering shells from some ancient dune.
And when finally he returns to here, earth,
For sure, you've got $6 million worth.

October 1977

Crabs à la Français

The French Crabs are very confusing,
Their Gaelic tongues quite intellectual.
Their culinary tastes are unsurpassable,
Their dress and manners completely impeccable.

They love their wine, which gets them in trouble.
A small carafe, and they're seeing double.
They look kind of cute in their chic berets
And other Français ways.

They are great lovers in true French style.
They're experts in the feminine wiles.
They have one problem that really shows:
How can you sound nasal when you have no nose?

October 1978

The Halloween Crab

A Halloween Crab climbed over the pumpkin,
Bobbing for apples he took a dunkin'.
He reached for the side and tried to grapple,
But instead, he became the first crabapple.

The Cowboy Crab

The Cowboy Crab with a ten-gallon hat
Is a legend of the Old Wild, Wild West.
With eight six-guns blazing, he's really amazing
When in a gunfight he is put to the test.

The Cowboy Crab, with his Texas drawl,
Has eight little boots and a pick-me-up truck.
He likes tobacco chewin' and cowgirl screwin'.
It seems like he's never down on his luck.

The Cowboy Crab has his silver spurs—
All eight that make such a clatter.
But his life ain't so complete as maybe you'd think,
'Cause one false move, and he'll end up on a platter.

October 1983

The Committee Crab

The Committee Crab is a busy person,
Wields a gavel with firm derision,
Belongs to clubs from A to Z.
In charge of subcommittees, he works busily.

He fits in well with the suburban scene,
Preparing motions to keep our city clean.
You'll find him at meetings most every night;
His gubernatorial docket is quite tight.

But for all the minutes and paperwork too,
There is one thing this crab can do.
He's not like typical suburban jerks.
This crab is unusual—he really works.

November 1977

Crabonomics

The Political Crab on the campaign trail
Will promise them anything—never fail.
But once elected and the campaign's past,
He will forget all of them oh so fast.

He's oh so elegant in the great debate.
He really believes he was given a mandate.
He kisses the cribbies and shakes the claws
And talks of the colony upholding the laws.

This cunning crab with the shifting eyes
Knows that eventually he'll get caught in his lies.
So he plans the opposite of a chief exec;
He'll retire from politics to the movie set.

November 1984

The Election Crab

The Election Crab goes to the poll—
Carter, Mondale, Ford, or Dole.
Those poor crabs don't have much to say
About the Washington crabs that they must pay.

The Election Crab makes his choice.
You've heard the crab-constituent voice.
They think that those jerks are all the same.
But then you won't have a crab to blame.

The Santa Crab

The Santa Crab came in a sleigh
With gifts for the crabs to give away.
Crabs love Christmas and holiday cheer.
They're full of spirits from ear to ear.

The Santa Crab on Christmas Eve
Crawls down the chimney with gifts to leave.
Old Santa Crab sure takes a-rockin'
When the crabs hang up all eight stockin's.

The Flying Dutchmen—
My Family

The Captain

A child was born on the California beach
But moved back east from the earthquakes' reach—
A quirk of fate, a seeming mystery,
That they settled to live in Sault Ste. Marie.
Scotch-Dutch by descent, American by birth,
A family of sailors, their lifeblood was made worth.
The lore of the lakes and the boats that sailed them
Pulsed through the veins of that entire generation.

This man was destined to be a sailor too.
He learned his trade, and too, it was true.
He grew in his skill and then took a wife,
Realized that sailing is not family life.
There was a job that could combine the two:
The home he loved and the locks of the Sault.
They both worked hard to build a home—
One that children remember wherever they roam.

The years were hard; there wasn't much money.
They did what they could, and you know, it's funny.
When life's seas are rough, true bravery shows,
But then, that's something that a sailor knows.
With a lot of work, and sweat and grief,
They instilled in their children Christian belief.

To educate their children, they worked through the years
And produced a nurse and two engineers.

The time had come to return to the lakes.
And as a tugman, he had what it takes.
He sailed the *Miss Lana* and *Bridgebuilder II*,
The *Harry S. Price*, and many more too.
When finally retirement age he did reach,
He truly earned his time "on the beach."
They were ready to enjoy those autumn years
And forever relax from those everyday fears.

But as we all know, we can't predict
What will be God's own and final edict.
There was meant to be more suffering done
From an illness whose battle couldn't be won.
That man who had sailed many countless seas
Was soon too swamped by this dreaded disease.
This was to be the last nor'wester.
And turmoiled seas calmed from that awful fester.

Epilogue

A sailor is born, and a sailor dies.
There are many joys and many cries.

Life on earth, for all it's worth,
Is well understood from a sailor's birth.

To my father: he was so much more than just a sailor.
—G. P. T.

November 1976

Erica—Christmas 1993

As with the magi who followed the star,
Your gift from us yet lies afar.
It's not under the tree, as you might suppose,
But is hidden in some other Yuletide repose.

So follow the clues as the wise men of old,
And your Christmas joy is sure to unfold.
The first place to try is where the Yule log slumbers
When the hot Texas air reaches triple numbers.

Well, you solved that clue; how clever of thee.
But the gift of the magi was not quite so easy.
So, the next mystery that you must solve
Will surely test your investigative resolve.

It seems to me that an appropriate cache
May be where Father hides his Yuletide stash,
Since during the cooler Texas days,
This item not used in a closet lays.

Congratulations on weaving through this mysterious plot.
I never dreamed you'd find this spot.
But in keeping with the mystery of Christmastime,
I must continue with yet another rhyme.

One place to look is an appropriate place.
Since the temperature's as cold as a snowman's face,
It also lies east of the Christmas star
And requires you to travel farther afar.

Finding this clue has surely chilled your ardor.
But the next, I fear, will be even harder.

For the gift you seek lies nearer than ever.
'Tis a place from which you chose to sever.
It once was home to thousands of threads
And, like the manger of old, hides in a child's bed.

Lil Sis

Birthdays come, and birthdays go.
And the years go by, and not so slow.
Our joints ache more each and every day.
But one thing is true, as I always say:
Though our muscles sag and eyesight goes,
Our humor stays, and my poetry flows!

December 2016

My Dad

You held my hand
When crossing streets.
When I was good,
You brought me treats.
On stormy nights,
You tucked me in.
You wiped the milk
From my chin.
And so this poem goes to you,
The one who helped me see it through.

—Erica "Annie" Ten Eyck

Polaris

Polaris—
Shining brightly in a clear indigo night,
Steady and strong—
Is guiding,
Safekeeping,
Leading.

Polaris—
Hanging watchful
In a noonday sun—
Is vigilant behind the gray clouds.

When the waves crash against me,
    Threatening,
    Tempting to lead me astray
    Polaris steadies my heart.

When I am directionless,
    Searching the ashen overcast,
    Polaris is my silent beacon.

When I am blinded by the glare of reality,
Unsure,
Polaris—I reach out my hands and feel the steady pulse in
my soul.

When I am lost in the blackest midnight,
> Unable to find comfort in the corners of my prison
> walls,
> Polaris, shimmering—a silver thread—
> Draws me in,
> Leading me home.

At dawn, Polaris heralds and celebrates the new day and its
infinite possibilities.
At nightfall, Polaris tucks me in—keeping watch over my
dreams.

Happy Father's Day, Papa. I love you to the moon and back.
—E. T. P.

June 21, 2015

Quintet in T

The oldest, Gary, is a boy real fine.
You'll find him running most of the time.
In addition to girls, he has a snake in a cage—
Ain't bad hobbies for a guy his age.

Wendy, too, never causes many troubles,
Chewing gum and blowing bubbles.
She digs rock music; it's always playin'
So loud she can't hear what you're sayin'.

Next comes Steve; he'll be okay.
He's on the go most of the day.
He's so darn active he keeps us running—
The only guy with outdoor plumbing.

Little Erica with her big brown eyes—
Gosh, she's loud whenever she cries.
She's a smart one tho, you gotta admit.
She does real well for having half a wit.

Cris, the caboose, is the end of the line.
Babies are supposed to be so divine.
He sure does scream, tho, when he gets mad.
But for a little dude, he ain't half-bad.

Well, that's the group; you've met 'em all.
Life for father, ain't it a ball?
My Lord, when I think of that motley crew,
I'm usually ready for a martini or two.

To Cris

Cris, I have loved your mother.
      I want no other.
She has made us a home;
      We're no longer alone.
She is all of my life.
      She will always be my wife.
And when our life is done,
      It will have been fun.

When you were conceived,
      Her family grieved.
They wanted you to die
      So they could cover up the lie.
Your mother saved your life,
      The one who's now my wife.
Your life began in strife.
      Son, you'll have a good life.

The first years won't be easy;
      People will be sleazy.
But Cris, don't you worry.
      Good things will come in a hurry.
Together, we'll build a family.
      Hey, just you wait and see.
Erica and Steve will be part of you,
      And I believe this always will be true.

Someday, you will come to know
      Why I can really love you so.
I'm not really all that strong,
      But I, too, have been wrong.

When to you this world is cold,
      When you, too, have grown old,
I hope you'll think you have had
      One helluva good and loving dad.

—Your dad

To Gary—

This note is meant to help defray
Part of the costs that you must pay
To buy for you a ten-speed bike
So that you can ride and not have to hike.

It's also meant to congratulate
That you learned enough to graduate.
You earned good grades in those four years,
Although those weren't my biggest fears.

Now, in the next four years, I hope you learn
How the heck you're going to earn
Enough to support not only you
But your father in a manner he's accustomed to!

Seriously tho, we're really proud,
And I'll say it in verse and also out loud.
This is a special day; it's really true.
And I pray the future will be good to you.

Written on graduation day by a proud father who just so
happens to be a poet.
—Your dad, G. P. T.

June 1977

To Rick

You probably feel that in life's deal,
Your cards fell out of the deck.
But, Rick, my chum, don't be glum.
You'll soon have your problems in check.

Life can be cruel, and not too cool.
Take it from one who knows.
But there's life to live and love to give
And faith to help beat life's blows.

Gerry Ford, you know, received a blow.
And now he's working for peanuts.
But he's a good man; he'll be on top again
'Cause, shucks—he's got real guts.

And the same is true of someone like you.
I know it as I know my own name.
They'll sew up your head, kick you out of bed,
And you'll be right back in life's game.

For my nephew, Rick Gulliver, who did not survive life's
blows—you are gone from your earthly lair but not forgotten.
—Uncle Gary

To Steve

Happy birthday, buddy, with boots so muddy.
You really look just like a boy.
You're getting tall, but above it all,
You really are a joy.

We're proud of you; it's really true.
You've grown so much this year.
You can be a chore, You ain't no bore.
But to me, you're very dear.

As you grow old, life will unfold
Into a beauty you've never known.
You'll be a good man, so I'll say again
We're really proud; you're one of my own.

March 1977

To the Italian Stallion

On the days before Christmas
And through this old town,
Being strapped to a bed
Can make you feel down.

While we are trying to shop,
We have all that holiday crap
Like hanging the tinsel
And those packages to wrap.

And as I sit by my fire
With my bottle of brandy
With Charlie by my side,
I keep my faithful pup handy.

So I pause and I think
When next year's holidays loom.
Maybe it will be my turn
To have blonds in my hospital room.

December 2016

Songs of Sandy

The Money Lady

There is an accountant, and her name is Sandy.
At her computer, she's pretty darn handy.
She keeps the books down to the very last cent.
As for expenses, she knows where every nickel went.

But there's more to this lady, a comely lass.
She brightens our day with a touch of class.
Her laughing eyes and dancing smile,
They warm our hearts for more than a while.

She is more than simply a money lady, you see.
The S in Sandy is what holds together U, B, and E.

August 2016

A Pup Named Piggy
and Her Mom

A pup was left on a road to die.
But a kind man said, "I'll save her or try."
He brought her home to his loving wife.
She said to the pup, "I must save your life."

The pup's eyes weren't even opened yet.
So she fed her a bottle; in her lap she was set.
As the pup grew strong and opened her eyes,
The vision she saw was a happy surprise.

The lovely face she saw could be no other;
She had to be the pup's own true mother.
She taught her to run and romp and play—
A game they still play to this very day.

But then one day, the kind man went away.
And my mom cried so and couldn't play.
I had to grow up and protect my mom
And would do so from that day on.

I was a pup no more, so soft and squiggly.
I was a grown-up dog; she called me Piggy.
For the rest of our lives, there will be no other.
We will be "Piggy the Pup" and her own true mother.

December 2016

A Thought of Sandy

Sandy, my pal, you are quite the gal,
And that is plain to see.
You're as cute as the bug in the proverbial rug,
And as pretty as a girl can be.

When we share our fruit, I don't give a hoot
If I finish my work at all.
Cuz when I'm in my chair in your office lair,
We really do have us a ball!

June 2017

Maggie and Pudge

Sandy, it seems when I write a poem,
Our dogs get all the written words;
But the cats are left alone to roam.
I have penned lines of Piggy and Charlie Chip.
Even a pup named Pepi got quite a rip.

So the time has come to pen a rhyme
About Maggie and Pudge an' give them some time.
The quiet lil cats wait patiently
To get a little time and notoriety.

So here's to Maggie without a tail.
Her furry body leaves quite a trail
Of fuzz and litter and hair balls too
And things we don't say, even though they're true.

And Pudge, of course, the little black one
Who harasses poor Piggy and calls it fun—
Her sneaky ways at the litter box
Create havoc, like a sly old fox.
So here's to you, you naughty feline,
Ruling over the house as a regal lion.

But alas, life wouldn't be the same
Without these cats and their endless game.
I hope it cheers the little balls of fun
And gives these cats a day in the sun.

"Meow."

April 27, 2017

Fruit Time

Of all the joys I have at work,
There's one that tops the list.
It's short in time yet so sublime.
The fruit we share is my best perk.

The night before, when I clean my grapes
And pack them in my lunch,
I know you'll have an orange to share.
It will be so sweet; I have a hunch.

It amazes me we have time to flit.
After the snack is gone,
And we've cleaned your desk,
We'll have time for us, before we split.

October 2017

A Lament for Pudgie

When I heard about Pudgie the cat,
I couldn't believe my ears.
It was the worst of all my fears.
I couldn't believe she was really gone.
So I did what I do best for her
And wrote poor Pudgie a song.

I thought of the black cat with a nocturnal way.
She roamed her yard as a feline does,
Skulking in her sleek black coat,
Protecting her yard, just cuz!
She teased her sisters
And gave them fits.
She could outrun poor Piggy
And with Maggie give her a "pszzzt."
I know Sweet Sandy; she was a special kind.
And like all living creatures,
She will live forever in this poet's mind.

Memorial Day 2017

A Song of Sandy, My Lady with the Flaxen Hair

She came to me as a fleeting wind
In my time of great despair.
Her laughing eyes and dancing smiles
Brought me joy beyond compare.

As our friendship grew, our talks did too.
We shared our joys and pains
Of our families and pets, those little idjits
That will forever fill our brains.

We shared our secrets, both good and bad,
And cheered us up when things were sad.
When I had problems that seemed not to end,
You helped me through them, and they lessened.

And then one night, when the moon was bright
With a hint of jasmine in the air,
It came to me, as plain as could be,
That you had become my lady with the flaxen hair.

And we became close friends, but not too close,
For that was how it should be.
I sit here now in my musings;
For me, that was plain to see.

And finally, when my work is done
And my time has come
And I must leave my earthly lair,
My final thoughts will be of laughing eyes and dancing smiles,
Of my lady with the flaxen hair.

July 2017

Printed in the United States
By Bookmasters